YOUR
BEST
MOVE

YOUR
BEST
MOVE

Effective Leadership Transition for the Local Church

ROBERT KAYLOR

Paperback ISBN: 978-1-62824-030-6
Mobi ISBN: 978-1-62824-031-3
ePub ISBN: 978-1-62824-032-0
uPDF ISBN: 978-1-62824-033-7

Library of Congress Control Number: 2013937022

Cover design by Andrew Dragos and Joey McNair
Page design by PerfecType, Nashville, TN

SEEDBED PUBLISHING
Sowing for a Great Awakening
204 N. Lexington Avenue, Wilmore, Kentucky 40390
www.seedbed.com

Contents

Acknowledgments

I am thankful for the opportunity I received to conduct this research on clergy transitions via a full scholarship through the Beeson International Center at Asbury Theological Seminary. I am thankful to the late Ralph Waldo Beeson for funding this program through his generosity and vision, which is enabling a new generation of pastors to increase their effectiveness in ministry. Drs. Randy Jessen, Tom Tumblin, Milton Lowe, and Russell West of the Beeson Center helped spark my imagination for the project, and Dr. Brian Russell mentored me through the writing process. I am also thankful for my classmates in the Beeson cohort, who are all great pastors and encouraged me with their laughter and prayers. Thanks to Chris Howlett, Antoni Sinkfield, Jane Riecke,

Diane Bell, Alice Wolfe, Steve Dunmire, Sabrina Tu, and John Whitsett, some of whom have already made moves to new churches themselves.

I have had the privilege of serving two great churches during this project, moving from a congregation in Park City, Utah to my present congregation in Monument, Colorado in 2010. Both churches eagerly supported my participation in the Beeson program and provided invaluable support for my family and me as I worked long hours on the project. I also appreciate the willingness of the pastors and churches in my conference to experiment with transition planning and give their feedback about the results they experienced in the midst of their pastoral transitions.

I am also thankful to my colleagues in the Rocky Mountain Conference for their enthusiastic support. The transition check-list and clergy covenant in the Appendix are based on their faithful work with pastors in transition.

I offer special thanks to J. D. Walt and Andy Miller of Seedbed for their encouragement, support, and guidance through the publishing process. Seedbed is a unique gift to the church and I am proud to offer this resource through them.

Lastly, and most importantly, I give thanks for my family: my wife, Jennifer, and our two teenagers, Hannah and Rob. They have endured several moves and transitions themselves, and while ministry certainly carries with it some uncertainty and change, they take it all in stride. Their love and support humbles me, and I dedicate this work to them.

Introduction

Early on the morning of February 25, 2010, I had just completed an epic workout at the local gym under the barking tutelage of my personal trainer. As I sat on the locker room bench trying to assess if all my body parts were still intact, I heard my cell phone vibrating from the top shelf of the locker—unusual for just a little after 7:00 a.m. I was pretty sure it was my wife, Jennifer, calling to let me know that I had forgotten something (a frequent occurrence), but when I answered, I heard the voice of my district superintendent.

Now in my own denomination's appointive system, district superintendents rarely call, especially that early, unless there's something big going on. That something big is usually the news that the bishop has appointed you a new church. There in the locker room, still breathless from the workout, I learned that I would be moving after seven great years at the church I had been serving. I had not asked for a move so it came as a surprise. So much for bringing the heart rate back down!

Whether you are a pastor or a church member, the announcement of a pastoral change is an anxiety-producing moment. Even if the move was expected, a sense of disequilibrium sets in when the theoretical becomes the actual. Whether they have accepted a call to a new church or been appointed to one, pastors know that a move brings with it a lot of logistical challenges, from getting to know a new congregation to getting a family settled into a new community. Churches wonder what life will be like with a new pastoral leader. Can she preach well? Will he care for me like the other pastor did? Who will officiate at my daughter's wedding or my funeral? The announcement of a transition immediately begets a whole host of questions and speculation about the future.

Like most pastors, I have moved several times over the course of a life of ministry. Some of these transitions have been smooth and some have made me wonder if going back to my previous life as an Army infantry officer would have been a safer and less stressful choice. No matter how many times you make a move, every transition presents a new challenge fraught with equal parts excitement and peril. While a move may present a great opportunity for a pastor to take on more responsibility, or a chance for a congregation to receive a new leader, any leadership transition also presents the potential for failure. Pastors and congregations both know the risk, which is why transitions produce a high degree of stress for everyone involved.

Michael Watkins, a professor at the Harvard Business School, says that transition represents a time of *acute vulnerability* for both the new leader and the organization.[1] The new leader lacks an understanding of the organizational culture, the working relationships of the people within that culture, and the organization's expectation of the new leader's role. Because of that lack of understanding, more than 40 percent of new leaders will fail within the first eighteen months of entering a new leadership role.[2] These failures typically happen when leaders commit errors within the first ninety to one hundred days of a transition, such as acting too quickly with limited information, failing to build key relationships and credibility with stakeholders, and not securing the few early successes that can lay the foundation for future success. The cost of that failure can be very high—up to twenty-four times the leader's base compensation according to one study.[3] Churches can expect at least a 15 percent drop in attendance and financial giving when an effective pastor departs.[4] If a church or pastor handles a transition poorly, particularly during those critical, first ninety days, the cost in terms of attendance, giving, morale, and momentum can prove devastating.

During my previous transition, I had not experienced that kind of failure. Things seemed to be flowing smoothly during the first few months, but as I reflected on it seven years later, I realized that it could have gone much better.

The church sits in the middle of a ski resort town and on winter Sunday mornings when there was fresh powder on the ski runs (which were clearly visible out of the church's windows behind where I stood to preach), the church would be fairly empty. Growing up as a kid from a blue-collar family in western Pennsylvania, this left me fuming for the first year or so of my tenure. After all, when I was kid I had a choice about whether I wanted to go to church—I could go happy or I could go sad, but I was going regardless. My congregants felt differently about church attendance, even when I preached on Jesus in Gethsemane and hammered his quote as I pointed out the window toward the lifts, "Can you not wait with me for one hour?" They waited all year for fresh snow because it was the reason they moved there in the first place. My griping about empty pews left us both frustrated.

It took me a while to catch on, but after some wise counsel from a few clergy colleagues in town, I began to see that my frustration was essentially a failure on my part to learn the culture of a ski town, where ministry happens as much outside as it does inside. When I started doing slope-side worship services at one of the resorts on Sunday afternoons, I began to see things differently. These people loved God, but on beautiful powder days they wanted to be outside on the mountain in a much grander cathedral. When I started to join them out there, they started coming to church in their ski bibs before heading out to the slopes.

I made a mistake in my early assumptions about ministry there, a mistake that could have proved disastrous had I not adjusted my approach early on. I did not want to make the same kinds of mistakes in this upcoming move, so I began to scour the Internet for books on clergy transitions. I found several, but they mostly promoted a "wait and see" approach to transition; warning against making any changes for the first six months to a year. When the district superintendent sent me the profile of the new church, the document said that the church wanted someone who would be a change agent. Most churches will ask for this kind of pastor, though their definition of change varies. I was replacing a pastor who had just retired after serving the church for eleven of its twenty-year history, so I represented change just by showing up.

I found some contrasting advice, however. Kennon Callahan, best known for his book *Twelve Keys to an Effective Church*, suggests that the best chance for new pastors to make some advancements and improvements happens in the early days of the transition, especially within the first ninety days.[5] If the first ninety days of transition represent the most dangerous possibility for failure, they also represent the best opportunity to begin achieving success. If a new pastor and congregation approach those first ninety days of ministry together with an intentional plan and a vision for success, they can establish momentum for change much earlier and begin developing effective habits that will lead them toward a successful future.

One of the books that I found most helpful in preparing for my own transition was Michael Watkins' *The First 90 Days*, where he defines the goal of a leadership transition as reaching the "breakeven point," or the point at which the new leader contributes as much to the organization as he or she consumes from it.[6] In terms of clergy transitions, a newly appointed pastor and a congregation reach the breakeven point when they have learned enough about one another, the church's organizational culture, and the cultural context of the community that they can then begin the process of casting vision and transforming the organization. The sooner the pastor and congregation reach the breakeven point, the sooner they will move out of transition and into the mission and future God has for them.

Armed with a goal for my transition, I began developing a plan that would include tasks for me and for the congregation I was leaving, as well as tasks that would help me enter the new congregation. Leaving a congregation that I had grown to love deeply over seven years would not be easy and we needed to deal with that grief together. I realized that the first task of transitioning to a new church involved leaving well from the old one. I also knew that the interim time between the announcement of my move and my actual first day at the new church could prove fruitful if I used it well. Using some of the material I had gleaned from Watkins and others, I crafted a transition plan that I presented to the new church. The plan involved several key tasks:

1. Leaving well: saying goodbye to my current church with grace and integrity and investing in the success of my successor.

2. Creating a Transition Team: bringing together a group of opinion leaders in the new church to aid in

the transition, provide me with feedback, and help me navigate both potential problems and early wins.

3. Achieving early wins: discovering the immediate opportunities to make effective and visible changes that would establish my credibility and begin generating momentum.

4. Researching the congregation: learning about the congregation's culture and its symbols, norms, and assumptions, as well as its emotional system.

5. Building the leadership team: developing relationships with key stakeholders among the lay leadership and team-building with the church staff, as well as clarifying and negotiating what the congregation, staff, and lay leadership expected of me as their pastor and what I expected of them.

6. Communicating during the transition: crafting a communication plan, which included letters, newsletter articles, and a blog to share information during the interim period before I started work, and a strategy for communicating during my first day, first Sunday, and first major change during the transition.

7. Maintaining balance: managing time well so that I could give attention to my young family as they transitioned into a new community, and paying attention to my physical and spiritual health during the transition.

The new church and I began executing the plan right after my introduction as the new pastor and I am convinced that the planning we did together as pastor and congregation enabled us to develop a strong relationship, navigate some potential land mines, discover some opportunities for early wins, and reach the breakeven point more quickly.

During my transition, I was working on my Doctor of Ministry degree through Asbury Theological Seminary. The transition plan proved so successful in my own move that one of my faculty mentors, Dr. Russell West, encouraged me to see if the plan could be taught and replicated with other churches with the same degree of effectiveness. I interviewed pastors and church leaders from ten different churches in my denomination about their transition experiences. The churches that executed the transition plan reported that they had effectively reached the end of their transition within three to four months of the beginning of the pastor's appointment. The churches without a transition plan still identified themselves as being in transition more than a year after the new pastoral appointment. The study revealed that a well-designed and executed transition plan is the key to a pastor and congregation starting well together. I continue to teach workshops on pastoral transitions and each year I hear from pastors and church leaders who have used the process outlined in this handbook to launch an effective new beginning in their churches.

This handbook emerged out of my study of various churches and my own transitional experiences. I designed it so that pastors and congregational leaders can use it as an easy reference guide for planning the transition together. The more the new pastor and congregation can share their thoughts, hopes, fears, expectations, and vision together, the healthier the transition will be. This book deals primarily with a situation in which a senior or solo pastor comes to a new church, but the principles can also apply to associate pastors and church staff who may adapt them for their particular area of ministry in the church. As you read through the book, you will likely come to the realization that there is a lot of work to be done in planning an effective transition, and you may be tempted to skip some of the steps. You will, of course, want to adapt the learning to your context, but I urge you to dig in and invest significant time in this process. The hard work you do over the first few months of your transition will make all the difference for both a good start and momentum toward the future.

If that phone call has already come to you, whether you are a pastor or a member of the church's personnel committee or lay leadership, I pray that this book helps you begin to work on your next move!

CHAPTER 1

A Theology of Transition

A pastoral transition is not just about changing leaders; it is also about furthering the mission of God through a particular congregation. Before we dive into the tasks that support an effective pastoral transition, we turn to the Scriptures for a look at how pastoral transitions can help the church gain traction toward the future. A solid biblical foundation gives us helpful tools to make good leadership transitions, which are important to furthering the church's mission of making disciples of Jesus for the work of God's kingdom.

The transition from one leader to another is a recurring theme throughout the entire Bible. Moses, for example, groomed Joshua to be his successor over a period of years, culminating in Moses' charge to "be strong and bold, for you

are the one who will go with this people into the land that the
LORD has sworn to their ancestors to give them" (Deut. 31:7).
The prophet Elijah anointed Elisha as his successor, leaving the
prophet's mantle behind for Elisha to carry forward (2 Kings
2:4–8). The kings of Israel and Judah struggled with succession
issues, with one generation often overthrowing the previous
one either by violent coup or, as in the case of Hezekiah and
Josiah, by overturning their fathers' apostasy through wide-
ranging religious reform (2 Kings 18:1–20:21; 22:1–23:30).
These few examples from the Old Testament indicate that
transitions in leadership most often occurred as the result of
a kind of apprentice-master relationship where the apprentice
was groomed—either intentionally or unintentionally—as the
master's replacement. Jesus would groom his disciples in a
similar manner, telling them that they would do even greater
things than he had done (John 14:12–14). Throughout the
Bible, God sends people to particular times and places in order
to further the mission of God's kingdom.

Pastors entering a new church setting might frame
their thinking and transition planning around the idea that
they have come to a particular church according to God's
timing, even if the initial circumstances of the change might
lead them to believe otherwise. If God has already worked
in the life of this church throughout its history—even if the
evidence appears on the surface to be scant—then a new
pastor must believe that there is divine reason why he or she
and this church have been thrust together for a season. The
first ninety days provide an opportunity for the new pastor to
learn where God has been at work and how his or her gifts

and skills can align with God's vision for both the church and its surrounding community.

In addition to knowing the times and seasons of the church's life and knowing how the new pastor's gifts and graces align with this particular time in the church's history, another theological consideration in pastoral transition concerns the missional lens through which the new pastor views the congregation's indigenous culture, norms, symbols, and relational style. While each pastor arrives at a new church with a particular personality type, leadership style preference, and theological worldview, the pastor must also begin to understand how the congregation will view his or her leadership through their own cultural lenses. The pastor must think like a missionary going into a foreign culture in order to understand the unique context of the church and its surrounding community.

Translating the message of the kingdom for people in a specific social context first requires an understanding of the culture of both the church and the community. The apostle Paul reminded the Corinthian church that he had adapted his leadership approach and evangelistic styles to the indigenous cultures of the churches he planted and encouraged in various locations around the first century Roman world. Acting essentially like a new pastor, Paul saw himself as a "slave to all," approaching each city and religious culture as a servant leader with an agenda to win as many people to Christ as possible (1 Cor. 9:19). Paul's own unique standing as both a Jew and a Roman citizen enabled him to connect with both Jews and Gentiles. He wrote, "I have become all things to all people, that I might by all means save some" (1 Cor. 9:22). Paul had learned to listen, adapt, and adjust to the cultural language of those he was trying to reach. Clergy entering new churches enter into new social contexts as well, and the early days of transition offer an especially rich opportunity to begin to learn how one's own unique giftedness, experiences, and cultural background might win people to Christ along with a congregation's buy-in for their leadership.

Whether the pastor is sent by the denomination or called by a local church, pastors are all itinerant messengers. We come to a church for a season, but there will always be a time to move on. As one senior citizen reminded me on the first day of my first pastorate, "I was here before you came and I will be here after you are gone." She was right! Pastors should see themselves as itinerant missionaries who bring the gospel to wherever and whomever God sends them. Two biblical stories stand out as examples of the kinds of appointments to which God sends itinerant messengers: Jonah and his difficult appointment to ministry in Nineveh (Jonah 1–3) and the seventy disciples whom Jesus sent on an itinerant mission to bring the good news of the kingdom "to every town and place where he himself intended to go" (Luke 10:1).

The Jonah story expresses the tension of arriving at a ministry setting where no prophet or pastor would have wanted to go. God calls Jonah to the hostile appointment at Nineveh, Israel's bitter enemy, while Jonah pines for the peaceful paradise of Tarshish, which lies completely in the other direction (Jonah 1:1–3). Eugene H. Peterson uses the Jonah story to point out that pastors can often see their ministry as a career where churches are used as stepping-stones on the pathway to success—but not success as defined by obedience to God:

> We respond to the divine initiative, but we humbly request to choose the destination. We are going to be pastors, but not in Nineveh for heaven's sake. Let's try Tarshish. In Tarshish we can have a religious career without having to deal with God.[1]

In reality, many congregations feel more like Nineveh than Tarshish: "a site for hard work without a great deal of hope for success, at least as success is measured on the charts."[2] Pastors sometimes find themselves in Nineveh, and must learn to rely on God's power and provision for the task of transforming the community while God transforms the pastor as well.

Luke 10:1–12, which describes Jesus' sending forth of the seventy or seventy-two, would seem to most mirror the kind of sending to a specific place, time, and type of ministry that pastors experience in coming to a new church. Jesus appointed seventy others and sent them to the towns of Judea as laborers for the plentiful harvest of people for God's kingdom (Luke 10:1–2). Churches may appear as emotionally dysfunctional wolves that can attack clergy who fail to prepare for the difficult tasks of leadership and change, while pastors may also be seen as interfering wolves who threaten the congregation's sense of security (Luke 10:3). The work of ministry has traditionally expected clergy to be ready to travel light, leaving behind the stores of good will and experience with one church in order to move quickly to a new setting. Such a call leaves little time for dallying or reflecting along the way (Luke 10:4). Clergy enter a new house of worship and church community announcing the peace of Christ. Some will greet this announcement with excitement, while others will greet the new pastor's arrival with reactive anxiety about the change of leadership (Luke 10:6). Clergy are called to remain with their congregations until released, receiving what the congregation provides even if that requires a lower salary than he or she received previously (Luke 10:7). Clergy are charged to be fully present to their congregations and not merely see them as stepping-stones to a different or more lucrative church "house" (Luke 10:7). The ministry of the itinerant pastor has not changed much since Jesus sent out the seventy—engaging in fellowship (Luke 10:7), offering healing to the sick in body and soul (Luke 10:9), and announcing the kingdom of God (Luke 10:9). Sometimes, too, Jesus calls pastors to announce God's judgment in places where evil and injustice seem to be the norm (Luke 10:10–12).

From the congregational side, the story of the sending of the seventy reminds Christians that welcoming the stranger often equates to welcoming God. Jesus sent the seventy ahead of him "to every town and place where he himself intended to go" (Luke 10:1), where they were to represent Jesus and his message that "the kingdom of God has come near to you" (Luke 10:9). Those who listened to the disciples' message effectively listened to Jesus and, by extension, listened to God (Luke 10:16). In the same way, in Luke 9:48, Jesus made clear that the one who welcomes him welcomes God.

The Scriptures reveal that God often comes as a stranger. God appeared to Abraham at the oaks of Mamre in the guise of three strangers who, after Abraham had provided them with hospitality, brought him the miraculous news that he and Sarah would have a son in their old age (Gen. 18:1–15). God appeared as a nighttime visitor to Jacob, and the patriarch wrestled with God until dawn, when God granted him a blessing (Gen. 32:22–32). The risen Jesus would appear to Cleopas and his companion on the road to Emmaus, coming to them as a stranger falling into step with them along the way. When Cleopas and his companion offered hospitality to Jesus, the stranger, they recognized him "in the breaking of the bread" (Luke 24:35). The writer of Hebrews offers advice to the early Christian community based on the divine tendency of God to come as a stranger: "Do not neglect to show hospitality to strangers, for by doing that some have entertained angels without knowing it" (Heb. 13:2). If a new pastor obeys the call of God to move to a new church, the receiving congregation should treat this new stranger and his or her family with the kind of hospitality that is worthy of the one who sent them. How a congregation welcomes a new pastor (and bids farewell to the previous one) reveals the congregation's understanding of hospitality.

No matter the denomination, pastors and congregations both know that leadership transitions will happen throughout their history of ministry. Managing transitions well, particularly in the early months of a new pastorate, can enable the clergy and the congregation to begin working for a larger harvest of people for the kingdom.

CHAPTER 2

Leaving Well

The announcement of a change of pastors begins a process that offers both crisis and opportunity, and managing the end of a pastoral tenure is a critical task for the outgoing pastor, the incoming pastor, and the congregation. William Bridges says, "The failure to identify and get ready for endings and losses is the largest difficulty for people in transition. And the failure to provide help with endings and losses leads to more problems for organizations in transition that anything else."[1] Unresolved grief, not putting affairs in order, and failure to let go of the relationship can derail the ability of both pastor and congregation to enter into a new season of ministry and can sabotage the incoming pastor's tenure.

The churches in my research study of pastoral transitions all stated that the number one driver of dissatisfaction in the transition process surrounds the failure of the outgoing pastor to really leave. When the outgoing pastor fails to prepare for the successor's arrival by taking care of basic tasks like updating important documents, preparing key information, and even making sure the office is clean and ready, the incoming pastor can find himself or herself at an information deficit, which will need to be made up before actually beginning the work of transition. When the outgoing pastor fails to really leave by continuing to visit parishioners in the hospital, or fielding calls of complaint about the new pastor, or even showing up in worship right after his or her departure, the incoming pastor then starts with an emotional deficit in the eyes of the congregation from which he or she may never recover.

Roy Oswald, who wrote some of the foundational work on clergy transitions for the Alban Institute, says that every transition begins with the emotional process of grieving, and we tend not to grieve well because we live in a "death-denying culture."[2] Funerals these days trend more toward a "celebration of life" than a recognition of grief in the midst of loss, and denying or avoiding grief prevents people from moving on with their lives. The same is true in pastoral transitions, as congregations tend to hold on to the memories of the predecessor and want to keep things just as they were. Pastors also deny their grief by failing to let go of the people and familiar surroundings of the church and thus never really leave even though they have physically moved far away. As one pastor I interviewed put it, "The real problem is that my predecessor's ghost is still here, even though he is still alive and well in another town. It's a friendly ghost, but it's still knocking around in every corner."[3]

Rather than denying the grief of loss, pastors and congregations do well to acknowledge that their relationship has changed. The best way to prepare for a pastor's departure is to use a similar process that the conscientious person uses to prepare for death. Think of it as a way of "putting your affairs in order" before the end comes. If that sounds a bit morbid, just remember that we Christians believe in a resurrection after death! Here are some of the ways you can begin to put affairs in order:

Craft a farewell letter. As soon as the transition has been announced, craft and mail a farewell letter for the whole congregation. The farewell letter provides a clear statement of the reasons for the transition and names the fact that the pastoral relationship is ending. Be honest about the reasons for leaving but do not assign blame, even if a bishop or some other denominational authority initiated the transition. Blaming the transition on a bishop, denomination, or any other person—or even blaming the will of God—is a way of avoiding your own role in the transition. If the relationship with the congregation was contentious and the change was initiated by the church's leadership, the church's personnel committee should carefully craft the letter while guarding confidentiality about the details. If the transition is sudden and unexpected, consider adding an invitation for members of the congregation to attend some listening sessions where they can voice their concerns. The goal here is not to defend or explain the reasons for the transition, but merely to listen to the anger and grief of the congregation.

The outgoing pastor should also clearly state the parameters of his or her relationship with the congregation going forward. Saying something like, "I will no longer be your pastor, but I will always be your friend" names the fact that you will no longer be in a pastoral relationship with the congregation. State clearly that you will not be available for weddings or funerals, nor will you be attending the church or fielding any calls about the church after your departure. You will help the congregation and your successor by defining the boundaries of your new relationship.

Lastly, a good farewell letter outlines the process of selecting or appointing a new pastor. Telling the congregation what will happen next helps to ease their anxiety and turns their attention toward the future.

A sample farewell letter appears in the Appendix at the end of this handbook. A carefully crafted farewell letter is a helpful first step toward dealing with the grief of transition.

Have personal conversations with those most affected by the transition. In any congregation there is a group of people who will be personally affected by the transition in ways that the average church member may not. Those who are near the end of life, for example, may be anxious that the pastor they have counted on for comfort and peace will not be there for them. Key leaders and people who have come to faith in Christ during the pastor's tenure may be disillusioned and wonder about the future. The outgoing pastor would do well to carve out personal time with those who grieve the transition the most, listening to their concerns, offering words of hope, and praying for the future together. The sooner these conversations can take place after the announcement of the transition, the more time these people will have to grieve and let go. Tears of sadness can often become tears of healing and even tears of joy. Pastors should listen carefully to the anxiety of the congregation and go toward it rather than retreat from it. Be clear, however, about what is ending while inviting them to imagine a new future with hope.

Prepare documents and information for the new pastor. Nothing is ever done until the paperwork is complete. Pastors who take the time to put together a packet of relevant documents and information for their successors offer those incoming pastors a true gift. The packet should include recent minutes of important meetings and financial status reports, church policy manuals, job descriptions, newsletters, bulletins, and other helpful information. I have found that including a church pictorial directory with notes about key people and relationships can provide the new pastor with a head start in learning names and beginning pastoral relationships. Also include a list of doctors, dentists, dry cleaners, and other local contacts that the new pastor might find helpful as his or her family transitions into new community. If you live in a parsonage, provide a separate packet with all the manuals for appliances, the phone numbers of maintenance and upkeep contractors, and a list of all the quirky stuff in the house, like jiggling the toilet handle and the like.

Putting this information on the pastor's desk in a clean office, along with the keys to the church, will go a long way in making the pastor's successor feel welcome and ready to go to work. Congregational leaders should work with the outgoing pastor to make sure the packet is complete. A sample checklist of typical items to include in the packet appears in the Appendix.

Have a "hand-off" meeting with the new pastor. Coupled with the transition packet, a meeting with the new pastor can also help bridge the gap and create energy for the transition. The new pastor will naturally have many questions about the church and community, and the outgoing pastor's candor in answering these questions will help the new pastor come in with eyes wide open. Incoming pastors should always reserve the right to formulate their own opinions, however. I once had a hand-off meeting with an outgoing pastor who made sure to tell me about all the people who would be out to get me. Those people proved to be my biggest supporters throughout my tenure at that church. Having a member of the church's personnel committee attend the hand-off meeting can help provide additional input from the laity side of the church. If possible, you may want to go through the transition packet together. If the outgoing pastor is fully invested in the new pastor's success, it will make the transition much smoother and bless his or her ministry with the congregation.

Craft a covenant agreement between the incoming and outgoing pastors. In order to mitigate any issues between predecessor and successor, consider crafting a covenant agreement that outlines the relationship of both pastors to each other and to the church. At a minimum, the outgoing pastor should agree not to interfere with the ministry of the new pastor, while the new pastor should agree to make no disparaging remarks about the predecessor. Some churches and denominational authorities have crafted covenant agreements that can be signed by both pastors as well as a denominational official and the chair of the church's personnel committee. A sample of one such agreement appears in the Appendix.

One of the things you might consider adding to the covenant agreement concerns a policy about the use of social media. Many pastors today have connections with congregants through Facebook, Twitter, and other media that can maintain connections even when friends are not physically present. How should a pastor treat those connections without necessarily severing all ties completely with people they have come to deeply love?

I still have social media "friends" from my previous churches, but I have also established clear boundaries for those relationships. I will not, for example, respond to any information, inquiry, or complaint about the church. I will also not respond in a pastoral way to any personal information posted by former parishioners except to refer them to their new pastor for support. I enjoy seeing news of babies born, graduations achieved, and changes experienced by friends from my former church, but I am no longer their pastor and must always tread carefully in those relationships. A clear policy on social media should be added to any transition covenant since this is where the greatest possibility exists for violating pastoral boundaries in the 21st century.

Conduct an exit interview. Exit interviews provide an opportunity for dialogue between the outgoing pastor and the congregation, represented by the personnel committee. A good exit interview explores both the triumphs and challenges of the pastor's tenure and provides the personnel committee with an evaluation of their relationship with the pastor and the state of the church in the midst of the transition. An exit interview can also provide opportunities for celebration of accomplishments and grief over unresolved issues. A sample of questions to discuss at an exit interview appears in the Appendix.

Consider a "passing of the mantle" in the primary worship services. One of the most visible and helpful tasks that can help a congregation and pastor name the change involves the participation of both the incoming and outgoing pastors in a joint worship experience, if that is possible. Like Elijah passed the mantle to Elisha, the use of signs and symbols can visually represent the change of leadership. Handing over keys or using a special ritual for the occasion marks the transition in memorable ways. When joint participation is not possible due to distance or other circumstances, the laity can help to bridge the gap. In one congregation, for example, the lay leader removed the stole of the departing pastor as the last act of the pastor's final worship service. The lay leader then placed the stole on the pulpit, where it remained for several weeks during the interim period. When the new pastor arrived, the lay leader placed the stole on his shoulders as the first act of their first worship service together. In another church, the incoming and outgoing pastors created a joint sermon, which ended with the outgoing pastor, who was retiring, laying hands on the incoming pastor and leading the congregation in prayer as they gathered around. That blessing enabled the new pastor to start well and have a long tenure at that church.

Many denominations have a ritual or order of service to mark a pastoral transition. I encourage you to use these or craft your own and invite your congregation to witness and participate in this vital act of releasing and welcoming.

Plan a farewell event. A good farewell event provides an opportunity for the whole congregation to say goodbye to their pastor with a celebration of their time together. Even if the relationship between pastor and congregation has been rocky, having a meal together offers an opportunity for reconciliation and peace. A good farewell event allows opportunities for both pastor and congregation to share witness and testimony of how their lives have been blessed during their time together, as well as an opportunity for fun. Some congregations will want to "roast" their pastor in fun, but I would offer a word of caution. Often what is said in humor and satire can have a biting edge and dredge up old hurts that this event should be trying to bury. Make the event as positive and festive as you can and both congregation and pastor will find it a great marker of the end as preparation for a new beginning.

Leaving well requires discipline and a great deal of work, but that work will pay dividends for years to come. For both the outgoing pastor and the congregation, an intentional process for leaving well allows time for grief and then an opportunity to turn attention toward the future.

Questions for Discussion

1. Which of these leaving tasks do you as pastor or congregation need to begin working on right away?

2. Who are the people most affected by the transition? Pastors, how will you approach them? Church leaders, how will you provide an opportunity to listen to them after the pastor is gone?

3. What will you do to mark the transition for the congregation? What ritual or worship experience will you craft or use? What shape will the farewell event take? Who will plan these experiences?

4. Pastors, how will you prepare for the success of your successor? Church leaders, how will you hold your outgoing pastor accountable to insure that these things are done?

5. Develop a timeline for leaving well, including the tasks above. Share this with the congregation's personnel committee, with the incoming pastor, and denominational officials.

CHAPTER 3

Creating a
Transition Team

Just as it is important for a departing pastor to take the appropriate steps to leave well, a new pastor should create a transition team to ensure the most effective entry into the congregation. The more people who invest in the success of the transition, particularly within the first ninety days, the better chance the new pastor and congregation will have at avoiding a myriad of potential pitfalls, misunderstandings, and unstated expectations that can derail a transition. A purposeful group of laity joined together can help the new pastor negotiate success early on and guide him or her toward the most important opportunities to achieve early wins that will create momentum and energy for their future together.

The Transition Team. A Transition Team consists of seven to twelve people selected by the church's leadership team or personnel committee. The members of the team should represent a wide cross-section of the church, including people of different ages and with various lengths of time at the church. The team should include several people who have the respect of most of the congregation, whether they serve in formal leadership positions or not. They should be positive people who have invested their time, talent, and treasure in the church and are excited about its future. The Transition Team should include one member of the church's personnel committee, but the personnel committee itself should not try to become the Transition Team. Personnel committees usually evaluate the pastor and staff and have a specific supervisory role that requires confidentiality in its deliberations. The Transition Team, by contrast, is an open group that solicits input from the congregation and communicates freely about the transition.

The best time to form a Transition Team is soon after a change of pastors is announced. The Transition Team can begin working with the incoming pastor to plan the first ninety days of the transition, including the events and tasks outlined in the next few chapters. The team can also help the outgoing pastor in the task of leaving well, though the personnel committee has the primary responsibility for the administrative aspects of the transition.

The primary purpose of the Transition Team is to facilitate conversations with both the new pastor and the congregation concerning observations, plans, expectations, proposed changes, communication strategies, and opportunities for the new pastor to achieve some early wins in those early days and weeks of ministry. The Transition Team demonstrates to the church that it wants to listen to people and provides a ready access to the church's "grapevine," aiding in the correction of rumors and misinformation.[1] It focuses its work on the first ninety to one hundred days of the transition and disbands after the pastor and the team mutually agree that they have reached the breakeven point, or end of the transition.

The Transition Team Process. The team connects with the incoming pastor during the interim period, between the previous pastor's departure and the new pastor's arrival. The new pastor and team craft a learning plan together (chapter 4) and begin planning opportunities for him or her to learn about the congregation. The members of the team should be introduced to the congregation during the interim period so that church members can ask questions and express desires or concerns about the transition.

Once the new pastor arrives, the Transition Team then schedules a series of meetings with the pastor at three- to four-week intervals which center around several questions:

1. What are you learning?
2. What are you hearing?
3. What expectations have been met or not been met?
4. What opportunities for success have you observed?

5. What "land mines" exist that could derail the transition process?

6. What is the next step?

Sharing information and observations helps both the pastor and the congregational opinion leaders to assess where they are in the transition and clarify any expectations. Expectations are like unspoken contracts that parishioners and pastors have with each other. Some church members, for example, may have an unspoken contract that requires the pastor to be their personal chaplain and call them whenever they have the slightest case of the sniffles. Others will have contracts about worship or preaching styles. Failure to honor these unspoken and unwritten contracts can cause a great deal of frustration in both pastors and congregants. The Transition Team helps to expose these contracts by naming them and negotiating their resolution, if possible.

The Transition Team also provides valuable feedback to the pastor before he or she institutes any changes. Leaders get into trouble when they make changes too soon without knowing all the facts and the potential emotional impact on the organization. The Transition Team can tell the pastor what changes the congregation will receive positively and what potential changes could cause an emotional earthquake.

For example, when I came to my current church I observed two things about the worship service that I believed needed immediate change. We had several people stand up during the prayer time every week and go on for several minutes about prayer concerns while the rest of the congregation fidgeted.

I asked my Transition Team if changing to a system where people wrote their prayer concerns would be an acceptable alternative. They said it would be welcome to most of the congregation, but also warned that it would cause some upset in a few members, namely those few making the requests! I made the change and when we heard rumblings of dissatisfaction, the members of the Transition Team backed the decision and worked with those who were upset. While the upset people did not necessarily agree with the change, they knew the reason for it and knew they had been heard.

The other aspect of worship that I wanted to change was the congregation's tradition of holding hands while singing the benediction response. I knew this had to be uncomfortable for visitors and, well, I am not a big hand-holder myself, either. When I proposed eliminating that tradition with the team, one of the members said, "Oh, you don't want to die on that hill!" This tradition went back to the church's founding and, even though it still makes me uncomfortable, we still hold hands to this day. The team thus kept me from making a catastrophic mistake early in my tenure.

A Transition Team is "almost like having spies," said one pastor who worked with a team during his transition. "It was nice to have people out there with their feelers out, figuring out what's going on and being able to address those problems and those issues . . . [to] build on the successes and change the things that aren't working."[2] Another pastor invited each of the Transition Team to secure a prayer partner from the congregation, which further expanded the team's reach and the congregation's engagement in the transition process.

Developing the Transition Team may be the most important step you take in preparing for a pastoral transition. Choose team members carefully and empower them to ask questions, give feedback, and be a sounding board for both the pastor and the congregation. And when you agree that the transition is over and you have turned your focus to the future together, take the time to celebrate the completion of the team's work. A team party is a great way to say, "We made it together!"

———— Questions for Discussion ————

1. Whom could you ask to serve on the Transition Team at your church? Keep in mind a diversity of age, experience, and constituencies in the church. Team members should be well-respected people in the church. List those names here:

2. Outline a process for the team's work. When will you meet? How often? Where?

3. What are some of the key issues you know you will face as a team? How will you negotiate them?

CHAPTER 4

Researching the Congregation

One of the key tasks that a new pastor must focus on is learning as much as possible about the congregation within those first ninety days. A pastor entering a congregation must take on the roles of historian, anthropologist, detective, and psychologist in order to understand how the congregation got to this point in its life. Each congregation also represents an emotional system with its own anxieties and assumptions about God, the church, and the role of the pastor.

Michael Watkins says that leaders who fail to diagnose and learn the culture of the organization will find themselves rejected by that organization in short order. He calls this phenomenon "organizational immunology."[1] Like a human body fighting a virus, an organizational culture can react to disruptive agents by isolating and attacking them until they leave. Leaders who act without learning the organization can trigger its immune system by creating the impression that nothing good existed in the organization until they, as the new leader, arrived with the answers. Leaders who arrive as learners, however, can begin to make changes almost subversively because they have learned the organizational system and know where the trigger points for anxiety exist. Leaders must learn to ask many more questions in the early stages of transition and avoid making statements based on uninformed assumptions.

The questions a pastor asks in transition should focus primarily on mining data about the congregation. That data emerges from several key sources:

1. Observation: What are the key symbols of congregational life? How do people interact with one another? What do they display on the walls or in the sanctuary? What is the central focus of the worship space? How are meetings run? What does the condition of the building say about the congregation? A new leader can learn a lot by simply observing the day-to-day operation of the church. Consider this as a form of ministry by simply walking around. Keep a small notebook in your pocket or jot a note in your phone every time you notice something, especially something that challenges your own values or assumptions.

2. Written records: Are the records kept up to date? Is there a written history of the church? Where are the records kept and who maintains them? What do the minutes of church meetings reveal about the nature of leadership and decision-making here? What does the budget reveal about the church's priorities?

3. Discussion with the keepers of the congregation's story: Every church has them—those old saints who have been around long enough to know how the church has evolved over time. Make a point to visit them within the first couple of weeks after your arrival. Listen to the stories they tell and bless their history. You will not only learn a great deal, but your presence will communicate that you value the church's past as much as its future.

4. Intentional conversations with everyone you meet. It seems axiomatic that the first people to make appointments with a new pastor are usually those with a particular agenda. They are quick to tell the new pastor that he or she is the best thing to come to the church since the gospel itself, which they had never heard while the other preacher was there. They just want to communicate a few things that the pastor "ought to know" about the church from their perspective since they seem to know what is best for everyone, including the pastor. They want to have the pastor's ear early on so that their agenda rises to the top of the priority list.

Without a clear learning plan, the new pastor can wind up making commitments or changes based on false or misleading information. The new pastor must beware of congregants bearing casseroles who offer praise and juicy information but conceal the instruments of the pastor's demise within their agendas. These people will almost always be the first to leave the church in a huff soon after your arrival, telling everyone who will listen how you have ruined the church because you did not take their counsel.

Most people, of course, will not come to you with such an agenda, but a helpful guideline for new pastors involves treating every conversation you have, especially those conversations with people you meet for the first time, as an opportunity for some proactive data gathering. One of the most effective ways to accomplish this involves setting up a series of gatherings in homes where you can meet most of the congregation in groups and ask them all the same set of questions. Think of this as creating a series of focus groups that will offer you, the pastoral researcher, a rich set of data to evaluate. While an all-church gathering is appropriate for saying farewell to a departing pastor, the incoming pastor cannot possibly have an opportunity to meet everyone and process their stories and perceptions of the church at a single large welcome gathering. The use of multiple home gatherings provides a better chance for the pastor to get to know the congregation and its people by the quickest and most helpful means.

Conducting Home Gatherings

This series of home gatherings should take place as early as possible within the first two to three weeks of the pastor's arrival. During the interim period before the new pastor actually begins work, the Transition Team or personnel committee recruits a number of people in the congregation to host these gatherings in their homes, planning for twelve to fifteen people at each gathering. The host family's responsibility involves only providing enough space to seat everyone in one room and offering some light dessert and coffee. Most people will readily agree to host these gatherings because they want to meet the new pastor while spending time with their church friends. The gatherings also provide the congregation with an intentional opportunity to offer hospitality to the new pastor by welcoming this itinerant stranger into their homes, much like those who welcomed the seventy missioners that Jesus sent. Once the hosts have been recruited, invite members of the congregation to sign up for the gathering closest to them or the one their friends will attend. Have as many of these groups as the size of the congregation will allow, keeping in mind that twelve to fifteen is an optimal size for each group. Plan for each gathering to last no more than two hours.

On the night of each gathering, the new pastor should arrive on time. Bringing the whole pastoral family along is nice, but families with young children (or even teenagers) will likely tire of the routine after two or three gatherings. There will be plenty of opportunity for the congregation to meet the pastor's family and this is not primarily a social visit anyway, at least for the pastor. The pastor is coming as a researcher with his or her own agenda and questions designed to learn as much about the congregation and its people as he or she can in a short amount of time.

Begin the meeting by sharing some brief introductions and stories. Ask each participant to introduce himself or herself and describe how he or she became part of the church. The pastor should go last and share a condensed version of his or her own story and call to ministry. This should take the first hour to complete.

During the second hour, the pastor moves the agenda toward his or her research project. The pastor explains that he or she has a series of research questions that will help the pastor get to know the congregation. The pastor asks the same series of questions at each gathering and takes notes on the answers.

The questions focus on the positive aspects of the church and are designed to get people focused on the future instead of becoming mired in the past. This is particularly important when the congregation has been through some turmoil and its people seem anxious about the transition. The questions emerge from an approach called "Appreciative Inquiry," which assumes that in every organization, no matter how dysfunctional it may appear on the surface, some things still work well. What an organization focuses on becomes its reality, and focusing on the positive enables an organization that is stuck to begin thinking about the future in a different way. When people focus on the good things from the past, rather than the problems, they will more likely carry those good things forward. The questions the pastor asks in the home gatherings are thus designed to get people to start envisioning the future while giving the pastor a snapshot of the congregation's past, its identity, and its hopes and dreams.

Appreciative Inquiry questions for home gatherings:

1. Remembering your entire experience at our church, when did you feel the most alive, most motivated, and most excited about your involvement? What made it exciting? Who else was involved? What happened? What was your part? Describe how you felt.

2. What do you value most about our church? What activities or ingredients or ways of life are most important? What are the best features of this church?

3. Make three wishes for the future of our church.[2]

Focus on one question at a time and allow the group to respond spontaneously, making sure that everyone has a chance to give their input. Jot down notes of important phrases, images, people, and events that emerge from the stories you hear. Do your best to move the conversation along so that you can finish within that second hour of the gathering. When finished, thank the hosts for their hospitality and the participants for coming. End with a prayer and an invitation to contact you if they have additional responses they would like to add to the questions.

The home gatherings require a great deal of stamina and focus for the pastor. I did eight gatherings in the first two weeks at my current church, which left me tired but glad for the experience. The upside, however, is that you will not only have gathered a lot of data, you will also have learned the names and stories of a large part of the congregation. The first time you call someone by name after worship, you will be glad for the experience and so will they. People are less likely to see the pastor as a virus if he or she knows them by name!

Once you have completed the gatherings, organize the data you collected and look for patterns of repeated phrases, words, stories, names, and values. Look for the important symbols, norms, and assumptions that characterize the congregation's self image. Identify the potential diversions and points of agreement between the congregation and yourself. You might organize the data around these three categories:

1. Highlights of the congregation's history.
2. The church's perceived core values.
3. The church's hopes and dreams for the future.

After gathering and sifting the data, prepare a summary report for your Transition Team and present it at the next meeting. Ask them to confirm or add to what you have learned. Invite them to share their own responses to the questions if they have not already participated in a home gathering. The goal here is to get agreement on some basic assumptions about the congregation as revealed by the data, which is important for the next step in the process: identifying and achieving early wins.

——————— **Questions for Discussion** ———————

1. What sources of information will you use to learn about the congregation? Who are some of the key

people with whom you should meet to learn the congregation's story?

2. How will the home gatherings be organized? What is the timetable for the gatherings?

3. How will you capture, arrange, organize, and present the findings from the data?

CHAPTER 5

Achieving Early Wins

The goal of a pastoral transition is to reach the breakeven point, or the point at which the new pastor adds as much value to the congregation as he or she receives from it. So far we have talked about tasks that lay the groundwork for an effective transition: leaving well, creating a Transition Team, and researching the congregation. The Transition Team gathers and evaluates the data gleaned from the home gatherings along with the pastor, but that data is merely interesting fodder for the file cabinet if it is not put to good use. Reaching the goal of transition involves a focused and intentional effort to apply the knowledge toward reaching the breakeven point, and the key to getting there is to achieve some early wins.

An early win is any short-term change, initiative, or innovation that offers the highest potential opportunity for improvement in organizational performance. Early wins excite and energize people who have been hoping for change and build the personal credibility of the change agent. Mostly, however, an early win creates value for the organization and when a new leader produces some early wins in the midst of a transition it can move the organization toward the breakeven point more quickly and with positive momentum. Failure to produce early wins, on the other hand, can lead to some people in the organization giving up on the new leader or, even worse, joining the ranks of the opposition.

Harvard Business School professor John Kotter identifies four characteristics of an early win:

1. An early win is highly visible. Large numbers of people can see the positive results.
2. An early win is unambiguous. No one can argue its effectiveness.[1]
3. An early win relates to the change effort in the organization. It meets the organization's goals or enhances its mission.
4. An early win rewards the change agent, undermines critics, builds momentum, and turns neutral people into active supporters.[2]

Think of early wins as the "low-hanging fruit" that can be had with a minimal amount of effort but with a maximum amount of return. Some examples of early wins that can be achieved within the first few months of a new pastorate include the conduct of a successful stewardship campaign that increases congregational giving or a bump in worship attendance during the early weeks after the pastor's arrival. Anything that creates positive buzz and increases congregational morale can be an early win.

Solving a long-term problem that many complain about but few have addressed is another opportunity for an early win. When I came to my current church, for example, I noticed that there was a distinct echo in the sanctuary that caused the sound to be very muddled, particularly when our musicians would play. Several of the older members of the church complained that they could not hear, and one said that he had not fully heard a sermon in more than three years.

As a musician myself (well, if being a drummer counts), and as the preacher, I found the problem distracting as well. I contacted a friend who works as an acoustic engineer and asked him to diagnose the problem. The solution involved installing acoustic panels on the sanctuary walls and adding a hearing assistance unit for those who needed the extra sound support. I dug through the church financial reports and found some money that had been given for another purpose but had not been touched in several years. I contacted the donor and asked if we could "repurpose" that money and he agreed. Within a few weeks the panels and wireless hearing assistance system were in place and working beautifully.

Now, this had been a problem that the church had dealt with since it had been built four years prior. It was one of those issues about which everyone kept repeating, "We ought to fix that" until such time as they simply began to live with it. It took an outsider coming in to name the problem again and then propose a solution that had no impact on the church budget.

After the problem was fixed, one of our oldest members came up to me in tears saying, "I finally heard the sermon!" I assumed, of course, that these were tears of joy and not tears of disappointment at actually hearing one of my sermons. He reminded me of that day again just before he passed away. It marked a significant early win for me in his eyes and many others. It was nothing difficult, mind you, just a simple solution to a simple problem.

That first big funeral, a wedding for the son or daughter of a church leader, even a good sermon on that first Christmas Eve can all be seen as early wins. If the congregation has been wounded by the previous pastor's misconduct or incompetence, simply doing effective basic ministry and keeping promises can be an early win. The more early wins you can achieve, the closer and quicker you move toward the break-even point.

Keep in mind, however, that your best source for identifying those early wins and testing their effectiveness is the Transition Team. They will steer you toward those early wins that will prove most helpful and away from other changes that could produce the opposite effect. Run the idea past them before you charge into making any changes, even if these changes look to be pretty simple. Remember, you do not yet know where all the land mines are buried!

In my research, every congregation that used a Transition Team process identified early wins as the key to reaching the end of their transition. Without a specific goal, pastors and congregations may take longer to establish their relationship and, as a result, delay their movement toward a common future. Planning for early wins as a means of achieving the breakeven point adds a sense of urgency to the transition process and helps congregations and pastors focus on the mission of the kingdom, rather than on the problems of the past.

Questions for Discussion

1. What are some of the potential early wins at this church? Discuss them with your Transition Team.
2. What were some of the early wins at your previous church? What were some of the early wins by the previous pastor at this church?
3. How will the early wins you identified help to move the pastor and congregation toward the breakeven point?

CHAPTER 6

Communication During Transition

"The single biggest problem with communication is the illusion that it has taken place," wrote George Bernard Shaw, revealing the truth that you can never communicate too much, especially when it is about something new.[1] The arrival of a new pastor represents a major change to the church's system of relationships, and communicating as much as possible with the congregation helps to bring clarity to the transition process.

A strategy for communication during a pastoral transition should focus on each of the phases of the process, including:

1. The announcement of the new pastor.
2. The interim period between the previous pastor's departure and the new pastor's arrival.
3. The pastor's first day on the job.
4. The first Sunday in the pulpit.
5. Before making the first major change designed to be an early win.

An effective communication strategy keeps the congregation informed and heads off potential misunderstandings, keeping the congregation's immune system from targeting the incoming pastor as an outsider and, instead, helping him or her to become more and more a part of the congregation.

The Announcement Phase. The announcement of the new pastor's name automatically creates a host of questions in the congregation and the sooner the congregation receives details about the pastor, the sooner the congregation can begin learning about him or her and finding points of connection. While a farewell letter is a vitally important first step toward a pastor leaving well from a congregation, a welcome letter from the new pastor provides an opportunity for the congregation to envision his or her arrival and the start of their future together.

Elements of a good welcome letter include a short biography of the new pastor (only about a paragraph), information about the pastor's family, a picture of the pastor, the pastor's plans for arrival, and a statement expressing both the pastor's excitement and anticipation about his or her arrival. Limit the length of the letter to one page as there will be more time to go into detail later and people will want to only know the basics at this time.

As with a letter announcing a pastor's departure, physically send the welcome letter to every member of the congregation so that even those who do not use a computer can read it. Consider publishing a copy of the letter in the church newsletter, bulletin, or on the church website so that visitors considering making the church their spiritual home will know about the new pastor as well. You may also reformat the letter into a press release for the local newspaper informing the community of the new pastor.

A major question that arises in every congregation when anticipating the arrival of a new pastor concerns his or her preaching style. If the pastor's previous church recorded and posted sermons online, adding a link in the welcome letter to those online sermons will alleviate some anxiety, particularly in congregations under a pastoral appointment system where the new pastor has not "tried out" for the position but is being sent by the denomination instead. If no online source is available, consider recording and sending an audio sample along with the welcome letter.

The Interim Phase. The period between the announcement of the transition and the new pastor's first day on the job can often extend for weeks or months depending on the denominational polity or local situation. This interim period offers a rich opportunity to plant seeds of good will for those first critical months of a pastorate. While the congregation should focus its attention on the outgoing pastor and managing the leaving process, some communication from the incoming pastor can help the congregation in its emotional transition by turning its attention toward the future while celebrating the past.

One of the most effective ways for the new pastor to communicate during the transition involves the creation of a blog (short for "web log"). A blog functions kind of like an online public journal for posting information, thoughts, editorials, and anything else the author wants the world to know. A transition blog focuses on the new pastor and his or her family and provides the congregation with updates and information in anticipation of his or her arrival.

The Internet offers many free sites that can host a blog, including sites like WordPress or Blogger. Whatever site you use, make sure they do not post inappropriate advertising on their pages. A new pastor does not want to inadvertently advertise commandment breaking before the first day on the job! Most web sites provide clear instructions for creating a blog, so even the least computer savvy pastor can put one together.

Plan to post information on the blog no more than weekly. Any more than that and it will draw your attention away from leaving well from your present congregation and overwhelm the new congregation. The best posts are those that provide the new congregation with basic information about yourself, your family, and the moving process. Some examples of effective posts include:

- The pastor's spiritual autobiography. How did you come to Christ and when did you experience a call to ministry?

- A "Frequently Asked Questions" post about your favorite foods, hobbies, sports, authors, etc. Have some fun with this!
- Posts about the physical move from one house to another. Update the timetable for the move and post pictures of the new house.
- Profiles of the pastor's family, including pictures.

A transition blog enables people to get to know the new pastor and helps them find points of connection. On the first Sunday at my new church in Colorado, for example, I received the gift of a Pittsburgh Steelers mug from a parishioner who grew up near my hometown in western Pennsylvania and knew that we shared a common love for the Black and Gold. He was excited to welcome me, and his gift allowed me to feel a little more at home in the midst of strangers. The parishioners from Cleveland were less excited to greet a Steelers fan, of course, but their good-natured ribbing was also a sign of their desire to get to know me.

Creating a transition blog, however, should always happen in consultation with the church personnel committee. Sometimes the circumstances of the previous pastor's leaving will require a more low-key approach. Most of the time, however, a transition blog offers a head start for both the pastor and congregation toward those critical first weeks and months together.

The First Day at Work. The first day on the job can set the tone for the transition. Start by moving into the pastor's office and unpacking all the boxes *before* the official first day on the job, if at all possible. A well-organized office with books on the shelves, pictures and certificates on the wall, voice-mail message recorded, and desk ready for action communicates to any visitors that the new pastor is ready for work. Congregations can help by making sure that the pastor's office is ready for his or her arrival, including clean carpets, dusted shelves, clear desk drawers, and fresh paint, if needed.

Pastors should also plan to use part of that first day to visit any hospitalized church members. These visits will not only offer pastoral care to the sick in the parish; they will also communicate to the whole congregation (and its grapevine) that the new pastor cares and wants to get to know them. Visits to shut-ins should take place within the first couple of weeks since they are often neglected in a transition and cannot be present for that important first Sunday.

The pastor will also want to meet with the church staff that first day, which we will cover in the next chapter. This first day offers a unique opportunity for the new pastor to make a lasting impression and demonstrates that actions often communicate more than words, particularly in a new environment where everyone is watching.

The First Sunday. The pastor's first Sunday in worship offers the first opportunity to see much of the congregation face to face. The first sermon, along with the rituals of transition described earlier in this book, enable everyone in the room to finally acknowledge that the transition has actually happened.

The first Sunday is full of both possibility and the potential for pitfalls. The new pastor knows very little about the congregation's way of worshipping and risks making unintentional faux pas that can make people uncomfortable. On my first Sunday at my current church, for example, I said the benediction at the end of the service and began to walk down the aisle toward the back doors to greet people, which was my usual practice. I was surprised, then, when the congregation joined hands across the aisle to sing the benediction response, as was their unspoken custom, and blocked my path—kind of like a liturgical game of Red Rover. I was a little embarrassed and wished I had known about that tradition.

That first Sunday can be awkward at best. I suggest that the only responsibility for the new pastor on that first Sunday should be preaching the sermon. Lay leaders or assistant pastors should conduct the rest of the service, unless something like a sacrament requires the new pastor's participation. This frees the pastor to think only about the sermon and not whether he or she is sitting in the wrong chair or giving the wrong directions. Some pastors have requested that someone else preach on that first Sunday so that they can observe the church at worship and then preach the following Sunday. This can be an effective way to alleviate the awkwardness. I prefer to preach the first Sunday, however, because I know we have both been waiting for that day. Allowing the church to demonstrate its hospitality and worship life while integrating the new pastor's preaching offers the opportunity for a good start together.

So, what should the pastor preach on that first Sunday? If the church uses the lectionary (appointed Scripture readings for specific days), the choice is fairly easy, though a mere elucidation of the prescribed text does not necessarily address the uniqueness of the day. Churches that use a series approach to preaching have more flexibility, but with that flexibility also comes the challenge of how to address the first day of what will hopefully be a long ministry of pastor and congregation together. There will never be another first sermon for this pastor and congregation and much is at stake in how that sermon communicates the future.

I have developed a pattern of using the text of Abram's call in Genesis 12 as a paradigm for ending and starting a new pastorate. God calls Abram to go on a journey where the destination is uncertain and, because he faithfully goes, God blesses him so that he and his family will be a blessing to the whole world. The church I am leaving is going on a journey into the unknown, and so is the one to whom I have come. We have been called to journey together: to be blessed so that we can be a blessing to our community and to the world. All that God requires of us is faith and the willingness to take the first step. So, when God calls, we haul, even if that means we leave behind the familiar and step into the new and the strange.

I often wonder if Abram was afraid to take that first step but did it anyway. As I stand in front of a congregation full of faces that I do not yet know, I know that I always feel a little bit anxious. "Is anyone feeling a little scared this morning?" I asked a congregation on my first Sunday. When they raised their hands, I was relieved that I was not the only one! In spite of our fear in the midst of uncertainty, we recognize that God has called us to the journey together. A good transition will help us get over that fear because the more we walk together on the journey, the more we will see it as a blessing that has come to us and will work through us.

Whatever text you choose for that first sermon, make it a message about new beginnings. Turn the congregation toward the future. Share some of yourself and how God has brought you to this place. Share your fears and your hopes. Most of all, share the promise of God who has brought you together for such a time as this.

The First Major Change. Sometime during the transition you will likely make a noticeable change in the way the congregation has traditionally functioned. The Transition Team helps to identify opportunities for early wins, but communicating changes is critical to get the congregation to adopt new ideas with the least amount of conflict.

William Bridges suggests that people need the answers to four key questions before they will adopt a change:

1. Why is this change important? (The purpose)
2. What does it look like? (The picture)
3. How are we going to get there? (The plan)
4. What part will I play in the future? (My part)[2]

Communicating the answers to these questions in writing and in person can help the congregation as they manage the change. Use newsletter articles, a blog, even a sermon to communicate the change and refer to it often. According to some experts, it takes at least six iterations of communication before the typical person actually hears the message being conveyed.

Remember George Bernard Shaw's quote at the beginning of the chapter: "The single biggest problem with communication is the illusion that it has taken place." When in doubt, communicate!

Questions for Discussion

1. Look again at each phase of the transition process. What is your plan to communicate during each of these phases?
2. Pastors, what text will you preach from on your first Sunday? What message do you want to convey?
3. Church leaders, what messages will be most important for your congregation to hear in the midst of the transition?
4. What modes of communication are most effective for reaching the majority of the congregation? What other methods can you add that may help reinforce the information?

CHAPTER 7

Building the Leadership Team

Building relationships with the church staff and key lay leaders is a critical task for pastors in the early days of a transition. The people with whom the pastor works most closely need to know his or her expectations of them, and these leaders want to express their own expectations, hopes, and dreams for the church to the new pastor.

The Church Staff. The professional church staff members are usually the most anxious people in the church during a pastoral transition. They know that their job security largely depends on their working relationship with the new pastor. Some old advice for transitioning pastors suggests demanding resignation letters from all staff members, which may or may not be accepted depending on how the new pastor views their value and place on the team. I have found that such an approach creates more fear than motivation and puts the new pastor at odds with the staff from day one.

Rather than assuming that the staff will not work out and then trying to prove otherwise, an approach that tends to bear more fruit assumes that the staff are invested in the life of the church and want to do their best to make the transition work. Yes, some incompatibility may emerge, but it is better to start with a clean slate than the threat of firing. The best gift a new pastor can give the staff at the very beginning is a set of clear expectations for their work while inviting the staff to clarify their own expectations of the pastor.

The time to begin clarifying expectations is the pastor's first day on the job. The first staff meeting offers an opportunity to not only begin building relationships by sharing one another's stories, but it is also an opportunity for the new pastor to be clear about his or her expectations for the staff and their work together.

For example, I have tended to have three expectations for staff:

1. I expect the staff to take initiative as members of the ministry team and do their individual work with quality and with the mission of the church in mind.
2. I expect that we will be open and honest with each other and that we will deal with conflict directly. We will not allow people to triangle us by complaining to

one of us about another staff person. We will always invite people to have a direct conversation with a staff member, and support any decisions that we make even if we do not all entirely agree.

3. I expect the relationship between the staff and myself to model the Body of Christ. We will pray for one another, care for one another, and support one another in such a way that the rest of the church will follow our example.

While I have expectations of the staff, I also want to hear their expectations of me. I want to know how I can equip them for their work and also hear what they want from me as their spiritual leader. Clarifying those expectations early, and even putting them in writing, creates a foundation from which the pastor and staff can begin working together.

Coupled with a clarity of expectations is a commitment to meeting individually with each staff member at the thirty-, sixty-, and ninety-day marks of the transition for the purpose of checking in on their adaptive challenges. An open and honest conversation about what is going well and what needs improvement allows for immediate feedback and evaluation of the team as you continue working together. If certain staff members do not adapt and changes must be made, the feedback from these meetings provides the data necessary to make the right decision without blindsiding the staff member.

Perhaps the most important role the new pastor brings to the staff team, however, is that of spiritual leader. Think of the staff as a small group of disciples that require mutual support and accountability, not only for their work but also for their spiritual lives. Studying Scripture or reading a spiritual book together provides a strong base for building a relationship that moves beyond work and into discipleship. Spend time in each staff meeting praying for one another and for the church. Get to know the team as people who not only work at the church, but as colleagues on a journey together.

The Lay Leadership. The lay leaders of the church also need some of the new pastor's focus during the early days of a transition. They want to know how the new pastor leads and how well they will work together. Carving out time to meet individually with key leaders of the church over coffee or lunch provides an informal setting in which to learn their stories and their perceptions about their committees and their role in the church. Three questions are helpful in these meetings:

1. What does your team or committee do?
2. What is your vision for this committee and how does it further the mission of the church?
3. How can I help you in your work?

Meeting with the lay leaders individually communicates that the pastor values their input and that the lay leadership really is part of the priesthood of all believers. If the pastor can start by assuming an equipping role rather than a doing role, it will pay long-term dividends as the church reflects the model of the Body of Christ and the priesthood of all believers.

Much like the relationship between the pastor and staff, the pastor and lay leadership should clarify expectations of one another as well. Expectations about the pastor's attendance at meetings, the division of responsibilities, church policies, and methods of conflict resolution are just a few of the topics the new pastor should broach with lay leaders.

Pastors should also monitor themselves closely as they attend those first meetings for each committee. Many committees want to always defer to the pastor for everything from the opening prayer to the vital decision. The pastor can help create an equipping environment by avoiding taking any leadership role in the meeting and by asking questions instead of making statements. Indeed, the pastor should function primarily as an observer in every meeting he or she attends, which adds another layer of data for learning about the congregation.

The best leaders are those who focus their time and attention toward building more leaders. New pastors must invest time in building primary relationships with both the paid staff and volunteer leaders, while acting as servant leaders themselves.

Questions for Discussion

1. For pastors: What are your expectations for the church staff? What do you expect from the lay leadership?
2. Staff and church leaders: What do expect from the pastor? How can he or she support you in your work?
3. Who are the key leaders the pastor should meet with as soon as possible?

CHAPTER 8

Maintaining Your Balance

In his insightful little book *Ministry is a High Calling, Aim Low*, pastor Kurt R. Schuermann equates the process of arriving at a new church to jumping on a moving train, while leaving the church is a lot like jumping off that same train a few miles down the track. Both events can be disorienting.[1] If that is true, then one of the most important tasks for a pastor in the midst of transition involves staying out from under the wheels!

Keeping personal balance in the midst of transition enables a new leader to maintain energy and perspective, make sound decisions, and care for his or her own personal life and relationships. Failure to maintain a balance between the personal and the professional can cause new leaders to fall into a vicious cycle of distraction that can derail the transition process. Loss of focus, undefended personal boundaries, brittleness or inflexibility, isolation, biased judgments, work avoidance, and chronic underperformance emerge as the inevitable results of unmanaged and undisciplined lack of balance.

Michael Watkins offers "three pillars of self-efficacy" that help to avoid these traps:

1. Adopting success strategies, such as developing a transition plan based on the tasks previously outlined, can provide a new leader with confidence and energy for the transition process.
2. Enforcing self-discipline, or regular routines, in both the personal and professional spheres of life provides a sense of balance and helps to monitor stress.
3. Building support systems among family and peers, as well as enlisting those who can provide wisdom, advice, and counsel, can provide a new leader with personal efficacy and well-being.[2] Clergy should surround themselves with people who will support and encourage them with equal measures of comfort and challenge. For many pastors, that frontline support system begins with their family.

Balancing Family. Some might argue that the first congregation a pastor needs to be concerned about is his or her own family. Pastors with families must remember that they are not the only ones transitioning to a new community, and their family's transition may generate more anxiety than the pastor will experience in dealing with the new church. Spouses and children may be leaving behind friends and familiar places, and younger children may be attending a new school. Transitioning pastors should plan to build in extra time to spend with family during the early weeks of the transition. While the schedule will certainly be full as you get to know the church, carving out time with each family member to discuss how he or she is adjusting will help them express their own feelings about all the new changes and people they are experiencing. Plan some fun activities in the new community, including those attractions that both locals and visitors like to frequent. Eat out together in a local restaurant. Plan frequent date nights with your spouse to listen to his or her concerns. Help organize the new house. Take the kids to visit their new schools and arrange time to talk with teachers. Do not place expectations on your family to be at every church event in those early days of the transition. That is your job, not theirs. Rather, do your best to help your family with their adjustment to the new situation at home as you adjust to your new situation at the church.

Single clergy may not have a family to get settled during the transition, but they still need space to learn the new environment. Churches should respect the boundaries of single pastors and not try to "fix them up" or intrude upon them without permission. Some congregations expect single clergy to work harder than their married counterparts, but that is an undue expectation. Single clergy need to begin developing support systems outside the church, and the church will do well to lend help only when asked. Single pastors, on the other hand, should communicate their needs clearly and state their boundaries in a loving way as soon as possible.

Balancing Spiritual Life. A significant part of maintaining balance for clergy involves attention to the spiritual life: "A strong argument could be made that a clergyperson's spiritual life should be her/his first job responsibility."[3] Most clergy understand the constant tension between church and family time, but fewer acknowledge the tension between the church and their own spiritual lives. Maintaining personal spiritual disciplines like prayer, Scripture reading, fasting, and solitude allows a pastor to maintain perspective in the swirl of confusion and newness surrounding a transition to a new church.

Pastors might consider connecting with a spiritual director or counselor as the transition unfolds. Sometimes a neutral observer who is not emotionally involved in the transition can prove helpful in monitoring feelings and anxieties as a pastor moves through the process. A group of clergy peers can also help in this way, particularly if the group consists of pastors who have recently transitioned themselves. Pastors who transition effectively tend to have a good support system in place made up of people who pray for them, encourage them, and provide them with a measure of grace.

Balancing Physical Health. The stress of a transition can take a serious toll on the pastor who is physically out of shape. The rounds of desserts at home gatherings and the constant pressure to be "on" can beget unhealthy habits unless balanced with regular exercise. One of the first things we do as a family upon moving to a new community is join the local YMCA or health club and commit to working out at least three to four times a week. Hiring a personal trainer or attending a regular exercise class will help hold you accountable to getting or staying in shape. Consider your regular workout as much a priority as your devotional time, which reinforces the biblical image that your body is the temple of the Holy Spirit (1 Cor. 6:19–20). A pastor cannot lead a church to health if his or her own temple is in disrepair.

Eating well requires discipline, especially in the midst of transition. Enjoy the desserts at the home gatherings, but only take a small one. When eating out, make healthy choices at the restaurant or the potluck. Eat at least one meal a day with your family, which will not only help you catch up on their experiences but will also keep you from scarfing down your food in a hurry.

Schedule appointments with your new doctor, dentist, and other health professionals as soon as you can after moving in. Put them on your support team and take their advice to heart as you work to maintain your health while working to make the transition successful.

Churches can help their new pastors maintain balance with their families and their spiritual lives by encouraging them to use their time well and take time off regularly. Some of the best words a pastor can hear in the first few weeks of a transition are, "We love you. Now go home!" Congregations that guard their new pastors' time and do not expect too much too soon actually provide space for them to devote their full attention to the transition when they are at work.

The Transition Team can provide some helpful monitoring of the pastor's time as the transition unfolds and can help communicate to the congregation that the pastor also needs time with family to make the transition successful.

One of the ways a congregation can demonstrate that they value the pastor's time outside the church is to provide the pastor and family with opportunities to experience the community on their own. When we walked into our church in Colorado on the first Sunday of July, for example, the congregation had set up a Christmas tree just outside the sanctuary. It was decorated with donated gift cards to local restaurants, ice cream parlors, unique local shops, and the local home improvement store. Those gift cards made us feel very welcome and gave us a chance to go out together and get to know the community and its hospitality.

A pastoral transition offers plenty of stress simply by being "new." Striking a balance between the personal and professional can be a key to longevity for pastors, and establishing good patterns early in the new ministry setting can turn a stressful situation into a fruitful one.

Questions for Discussion

1. What does the pastor's family need from him or her during the transition?
2. What boundaries will be helpful for the pastor to maintain as he or she begins work?

3. What spiritual disciplines will the pastor rely on during the transition?
4. Who does the pastor rely on for support? Who else can lend support during the transition?
5. What will the congregation provide to help the pastor and family get to know the community?

CHAPTER 9

Reaching the
Breakeven Point

When a new President of the United States is inaugurated in January after winning a November election, he will usually receive his first informal report card from the media and the pundits after the first one hundred days in office. That report card often sticks with a President until the next election cycle, four years later, when the voters will decide whether or not the President has been effective in leading the country. Those first hundred days give voters time to form opinions and offer a stark reminder that none of us ever gets a second chance to make a first impression.

If the President gets a hundred days to make an impression, pastors usually get a little less time before early opinions are formed that can make or break the pastor's tenure. Pastors and church leaders must be diligent and intentional in making those first weeks and months as successful as possible in order to turn the congregation's attention away from evaluation and toward excitement about the future.

We began this book by talking about the breakeven point as the goal of transition—the point at which the new pastor has contributed as much value to the congregation as he or she has received from it. The breakeven point in pastoral transitions relates directly to the transition planning process and the achievement of early wins. Transition planning leads to the identification and achievement of early wins and allows the new pastor to add value to the congregation, resulting in reaching the breakeven point more quickly. The quicker the pastor and congregation reach the breakeven point, the quicker they can begin focusing on the future together. Planning for early wins as a means of achieving the breakeven point adds a sense of urgency to the transition process and helps congregations and pastors focus on the mission of the kingdom, rather than on the problems of the past.

My research revealed that pastors and congregations generally define the breakeven point by the presence of early wins that solve long-standing problems in the church. Churches that begin to see some of these problems resolved will experience a shift of focus and identity and tend to credit the new leader as the catalyst for the change. The most effective pastors are those who help solve problems and generate momentum so people can focus on the future and on the church's mission as soon as possible. A good transition helps a pastor and church create a new identity together—one that can help add value to God's kingdom.

When Jesus sent the seventy out into the mission field, he commissioned them to add value and change the identity of people who had long been participant to the problems of disease, evil, injustice, and death. Jesus expected them to move people from a focus on the past to a vision of the present-future kingdom, proclaiming, "The kingdom of God has come near to you" (Luke 10:9). Effective clergy transitions focus on reaching the point at which the congregation begins to see a new future, with the kingdom of God as its ultimate goal.

Planning and working toward an effective transition takes a lot of work by a lot of people, but every hour invested by pastors, Transition Teams, and church leaders in those first days and weeks will pay huge dividends for both the pastor and congregation and, by extension, to the community in which the church lives and works for the glory of God and God's kingdom. When that call comes, I pray you will be confident that your next move will be a good one!

Appendix

Sample Farewell Letter

Dear Church Members and Friends,

On Sunday, March 14, an announcement was made at both worship services that I have received a new pastoral appointment/call to a new church (briefly describe church and its potential).

I write to you today not only with a deep sense of sadness that our time together as pastor and congregation is ending after a number of fruitful years but also with excitement about the potential for both my new church and for this church. (Briefly state reasons for leaving.)

The personnel committee is working to create a profile that will be used to match the best pastoral leader with the needs of the church. Your personnel committee, led by (name), is an outstanding, thoughtful, and professional group and will represent the church well in this process. Pray for them, and please contact a member of the team if you have questions or concerns. I have included a list of their names with this letter.

My last Sunday in the pulpit will be (date), after which I will use my remaining vacation days to make the move and prepare for my first day on the job, which will be (date). This will also allow time for the church to prepare the parsonage for a new family and for the congregation to catch its collective breath before welcoming the new pastor. The personnel committee will be working to provide pastoral coverage during the interim weeks between my departure and the new pastor's first Sunday, which will be (date).

As of (date), our relationship as pastor and congregation will change dramatically. While I will always be your friend, I will no longer be your pastor. I will no longer be available to you for weddings, funerals, or other events. You will soon have a new pastor who will have the privilege of being involved in the lives of the people of this great congregation in so many ways. I ask that you do your absolute best to welcome your new pastoral leader and help him or her in the process of beginning a new season of ministry together.

Times like this remind us that change is difficult, but it is also a constant part of life. The good news is that change also brings with it an opportunity for growth and new possibilities. I fully believe that God is at work in the midst of the changes here and that this church's best days are still ahead. I am already praying every day for the success of my successor and for you in the midst of this transition. I would covet your prayers for my family and the people of (new church) as well. By managing this transition well, with God's help, everyone involved will be further strengthened for the common work we engage in for God's Kingdom.

In Christ,
Your Pastor

Checklist for a Transition Packet

The following information should be included in the transition packet that the outgoing pastor gives to the incoming pastor. This list is not meant to be exhaustive, but will help you begin to gather the basics that will help the new pastor during the transition.

Documents to include:
- Copy of the church's vision/mission statement
- Most recent minutes of all-church conferences or meetings
- Church directory, annotated with information about relationships, pastoral care needs, and potential leaders
- Church email list
- Organizational chart and list of church lay leaders and committee members
- Church policies for weddings, funerals, building use, employee handbook, etc.
- Current and last two years of budget reports
- Latest month's financial statement
- Last three church newsletters
- Recent bulletins for each worship service
- Bulletins for most recent Christmas Eve and Easter services, as well as other special services that are routinely part of the church's life
- Church keys

- If the pastor lives in a parsonage, include the manual for all appliances as well as names and phone numbers of plumbers, electricians, snow removal, trash service, etc.

Questions to answer (either in writing or during the hand-off meeting)

Organization
- Are any staff positions currently vacant?
- Are any staff changes needed or expected?
- Describe any organizational process or structure that is unique to this congregation.
- What agencies or resources are available for those who may call with needs for emergency food, clothing, shelter, or assistance?
- Is there a ministerial association in the community? Provide contact information.

Financial
- What is the normal stewardship process at this church?
- Who is in charge of promoting stewardship in the church?
- What is the number of pledging and non-pledging households?
- What is the average financial contribution of each member family to the church?
- What is the pastor's expected role in stewardship campaigns?
- Does the church have a permanent endowment fund? What is it used for and how is it funded?

Technology

- Describe the church's computer network. Is it wireless? Is the pastor provided with a computer? What kind?
- Does the church communicate with the congregation primarily by email?
- Does the church have a web page and, if so, who maintains it?
- What are the appropriate passwords the pastor needs to know? How will the pastor's email be set up?
- Who knows about the church's membership and financial software?

Communications

- What is the church's primary method of communication with its members? What percentage of the church membership uses electronic communication (email, text, internet, etc.)?
- How often does the church newsletter come out? How is it distributed? What does the pastor need to prepare for the newsletter?
- How does the church communicate with the community? What kind of advertising does the church do?

Worship

- Who is involved in planning worship?
- What are the times of all the worship services?
- Are any new services being planned?
- What is the role of clergy and laity at each service?

- What is the average worship attendance at all services? Is it increasing or decreasing? Why?
- What is the role of children and youth in worship? Is there children's worship during the main worship services? Is there a children's message in the service? Who does the children's message?
- What styles of worship are currently being offered?
- How is the bulletin prepared? Who is involved? What is the timeline for completion of the bulletin each week?
- How does the church conduct the sacraments? When is communion offered and by what means?
- Are there ecumenical community worship events? When?

Pastoral Care

- What families are currently experiencing loss, illness, or special needs?
- Who are the homebound members? Is there a regular ministry in place for them?

Building

- How are building items and maintenance handled? Who orders supplies? Is there a custodian? What are his/her hours?
- What community groups use the building?

Exit Interview Questions

The questions below are just a few of the kinds of questions that personnel committees can ask of a departing pastor at an exit interview. The interview is a great way to express appreciation and also recognize the broken places in the relationship between pastor and congregation.

1. What do you believe to be your major accomplishments at this church?
2. What will you miss about your ministry here? What will you not miss?
3. What unfinished business do you feel you are leaving behind?
4. What challenges does this church face as it moves into a new season of ministry?
5. What opportunities does this church need to exploit as it moves into a new season of ministry?
6. How did this congregation bless you and your family? What could we have done better?
7. What was the best thing about serving here?
8. What was the most difficult thing about serving here?
9. How can we best support your successor?
10. Who are the people who will feel your absence the most?
11. What wounds have you received here that still require healing? How can we heal together?
12. How can we best celebrate your ministry as you prepare to depart?

Sample Clergy Covenant

This document provides both the incoming and outgoing pastors with a clear definition of the relationship between the pastors and the church after the transition has taken place. You can modify this to fit your local situation or church polity. The covenant should be signed by both the incoming and outgoing pastors and the chair of the church's personnel committee.

As clergy in covenant with one another, and in the best interests of the church, we covenant to follow these guidelines as the pastoral transition takes place:

1. Make no disparaging remarks about the work or lifestyle of a predecessor, successor, or other ministers.
2. Perform no pastoral functions in any church the pastor no longer serves, except at the request and under direction of the pastor in charge.
3. Upon leaving the church, including retirement, sever pastoral relationships with the congregation, recognizing that all future weddings, baptisms, counseling sessions, visitations, and funerals should be fulfilled by the current pastor, unless an unusual situation exists and is approved by the current pastor. When receiving a request from a former parishioner, the preceding pastor will always refer them, without comment, to the current pastor. The former pastor can only participate in a church event if invited by the current pastor.

4. If the former pastor still resides in the same community after leaving the church, the former pastor and family must find another church to attend. The former pastor's continued presence in the congregation almost always hinders the congregation and its current pastor from developing the necessary relationship for successful ministry. We realize that this can be painful for the former pastor and family, but the best interests of everyone involved are best served by this policy. Reconsideration of this policy may occur after the former pastor has been absent a minimum of one year, but only in consultation with the personnel committee and the current pastor.

5. The former pastor shall avoid all conversation and communication with church members about the new pastor, as well as problems and issues regarding the former church. If approached, the former pastor needs to explain that ministerial ethics does not permit such a discussion.

6. Continued personal relationships with congregants do not assist the health and welfare of the local church and are therefore discouraged. Pastors may maintain contact with former congregants at a distance through such means as social media, but must be clear that these relationships are not of a pastoral nature and that discussions about the church or its current pastor are not permissible.

7. Before leaving, the exiting pastor will communicate clearly from the pulpit and in writing that he or she

will no longer be able to function in any pastoral way with the congregation.

8. The current pastor is also expected to be sensitive, gracious, and appropriately inclusive of former pastors, using the guidelines above.

_____

Date

_____

Incoming Pastor

_____

Outgoing Pastor

_____

Chairperson, Church Personnel Committee

_____

Denominational Representative

Notes

Introduction

1. Michael Watkins, *The First 90 Days: Critical Strategies for New Leaders at All Levels* (Boston: Harvard Business Review Press, 2003), 1.

2. Ira M. Levin, "New Leader Assimilation Process: Accelerating New Role-Related Transitions," *Consulting Psychology Journal: Practice and Research* 62.1 (2010): 61.

3. Levin, "New Leader Assimilation Process," 57.

4. Carolyn Weese and J. Russell Crabtree, *The Elephant in the Boardroom: Speaking the Unspoken about Pastoral Transitions* (San Francisco: Jossey-Bass, 2004), 30.

5. Kennon L. Callahan, *A New Beginning for Pastors and Congregations: Building an Excellent Match upon Your Shared Strengths* (San Francisco: Jossey-Bass, 1999), 85.

6. Watkins, *The First 90 Days*, 2.

Chapter 1: A Theology of Transition

1. Eugene H. Peterson *Under the Unpredictable Plant: An Exploration in Vocational Holiness* (Grand Rapids: William B. Eerdmans Publishing Company, 1992), 16.

2. Peterson, *Under the Unpredictable Plant*, 16.

Chapter 2: Leaving Well

1. William Bridges *Managing Transitions: Making the Most of Change*, 2nd ed. (Cambridge: Da Capo Lifelong Books, 2003), 8.

2. Roy M. Oswald *Running through Thistles: Terminating a Ministerial Relationship with a Parish* (Herndon, VA: Alban Institute, 1998), 1.

3. Robert A. Kaylor *Your Next Move: Planning for Clergy Transitions* (Diss., Asbury Theological Seminary, 2012), 98.

Chapter 3: Creating a Transition Team

1. Bridges, *Managing Transitions*, 49.
2. Kaylor, *Your Next Move*, 113.

Chapter 4: Researching the Congregation

1. Watkins, *The First 90 Days*, 94.
2. Mark Lau Branson *Memories, Hopes, and Conversations: Appreciative Inquiry and Congregational Change* (Herndon, VA: Alban Institute, 2004), 58.

Chapter 5: Achieving Early Wins

1. John P. Kotter *Leading Change* (Boston: Harvard Business Review Press, 1994), 122.
2. Kotter, *Leading Change*, 123.

Chapter 6: Communication During Transition

1. Marlene Caroselli *Leadership Skills for Managers* (New York: McGraw-Hill, 2000), 71.
2. Bridges, *Managing Transitions*, 58.

Chapter 8: Maintaining Balance

1. Kurt R. Schuermann *Ministry is a High Calling (Aim Low): Reflections of a Parish Novice* (Louisville, KY: Geneva Press, 2001), 15.

2. Watkins, *The First 90 Days*, 211.

3. Roy M. Oswald *New Beginnings: A Pastorate Start Up Workbook* (Herndon, VA: Alban Institute, 1989), 61.

Resources

Branson, Mark Lau. *Memories, Hopes, and Conversations: Appreciative Inquiry and Congregational Change.* Herndon, VA: Alban Institute, 2004.

Bridges, William. *Managing Transitions: Making the Most of Change.* 2nd ed. Cambridge: Da Capo Lifelong Books, 2003.

Callahan, Kennon L. *A New Beginning for Pastors and Congregations: Building an Excellent Match upon Your Shared Strengths.* San Francisco: Jossey-Bass, 1999.

Caroselli, Marlene. *Leadership Skills for Managers.* New York: McGraw-Hill, 2000.

Kaylor, Robert A. *Your Next Move: Planning for Clergy Transitions.* Diss. Asbury Theological Seminary, 2012.

Levin, Ira M. "New Leader Assimilation Process: Accelerating New Role-Related Transitions." *Consulting Psychology Journal: Practice and Research* 62.1 (2010): 56–72. *PsycARTICLES.* Web. 3 Feb. 2011.

Oswald, Roy M. *New Beginnings: A Pastorate Start Up Workbook.* Herndon, VA: Alban Institute, 1989.

———. *Running through Thistles: Terminating a Ministerial Relationship with a Parish.* Herndon, VA: Alban Institute, 1998.

Peterson, Eugene H. *Under the Unpredictable Plant: An Exploration in Vocational Holiness.* Grand Rapids: William B. Eerdmans Publishing Company, 1992.

Schuermann, Kurt R. *Ministry is a High Calling (Aim Low): Reflections of a Parish Novice.* Louisville, KY: Geneva Press, 2001.

Watkins, Michael. *The First 90 Days: Critical Strategies for New Leaders at All Levels.* Boston: Harvard Business Review Press, 2003.

Weese, Carolyn, and J. Russell Crabtree. *The Elephant in the Boardroom: Speaking the Unspoken about Pastoral Transitions.* San Francisco: Jossey-Bass, 2004.